The Underside of Things

First published 2020 by The Hedgehog Poetry Press

Published in the UK by
The Hedgehog Poetry Press
5, Coppack House
Churchill Avenue
Clevedon
BS21 6QW

www.hedgehogpress.co.uk

ISBN: 978-1-913499-44-0

9 8 7 6 5 4 3 2 1

A CIP Catalogue record for this book is available from the British Library.

The Underside of Things

by

Jenna Plewes

Contents

for Claire

LEARNING TO GO WITH THE FLOW

I can do this –

step in carefully
at the shallow end
test the water
get used to the cold
take a step
up to my ankles
focus on the next step
go in a little deeper
up to my knees
stroke my hands through the water
wet my arms, my shoulders
don't look at the deep end yet
go a bit deeper
step by step
water up to my chin
but my feet are still on the bottom

I know I can do this –

push forward,
the water will hold me
if I don't thrash about
turn on my back
look up
count the tiles on the ceiling
one by one

I'm in the deep end
floating
keep counting the tiles
one
by one
by one.

LOVE WILL BE OUR BEDROCK

We are separate, but we stand
on the same greening earth.

Around us life is busy, a song thrush
trickles shining drops, a crow

on the crown of a Monterey pine
rasps its black throat, a buzzard circles.

Hedges are white with blackthorn blossom,
celandine brighten the lanes, lambs grow strong.

City sounds are muffled, streets deserted.
Fingers send messages, smile greets smile on screen.

Fear prowls the tunnels of our dreams,
casts giant shadows on our bedroom walls,

but morning comes, we watch another sunrise
lighten the day, make a list of friends to ring.

WAITING

The quiet is uncanny, we float
a breathing sea of unknowing,
each wave drawing back then
spreading a thin skin on the sand.

A couple with a dog step off the path,
turn sideways as I pass. We do not speak
but we look back and smile.
A runner passes, waves as he runs on.

In bedsits and in city high-rise flats
televisions flicker, ringtones call,
children play their games on line,
tempers sometimes flare, hours limp by.

Each evening as the sun goes down
I watch the horses racing round the field,
clods of earth flying, long tails streaming.

In dreams I run, wind in my hair,
sand smooth and cool under my feet,
and find my eyes are wet when I wake up.

I'M SPRING CLEANING MY LIFE

wiping the diary clean,
taking down the calendar,
scrubbing dates and future plans,

unpinning notes of wishful thinking,
rubbing out regrets, outdated dreams.

Instead

I'm pinning up a photo of us all
laughing together, squinting in the sun.

I'm finding projects at the back of cupboards,
washing off the dust, revealing possibilities.
Tomorrow I'll choose one - make a start.

THURSDAY NIGHTS AT 8PM

There was a scatter of stars that first night,
the moon just a sliver of silver. We waited

for the signal. Then the sound of clapping
rustled in the darkness like a million birds

flying from doorways and windows of cottages,
from high-rise flats, farmhouses and narrowboats.

Minute followed minute, then they were gone.
We shut our windows, went inside, but the air

felt different. The birds had taken something precious
into the night sky and given something precious back.

COFFEE TIME - ON LINE

Your face fills my screen; slightly out of focus
mine's a postage stamp in the right-hand corner,
I'm at the kitchen table; you're by the sink.

You boil the kettle; choose your favourite mug.
I have the blue tin, take out my teabag,
you spoon out coffee, mine's green tea, no milk.

We meet in no-man's land, smile matching smile –
you watch yourself watching me, I do the same.
I want to shut it out; that little face catching

my attention, drawing me away from you
back to my messy hair that needs a cut,
the shirt that should be washed today.

I want to read your face, both of us on the same
page sharing the story of our separate days, laughing,
solitary; but not alone, reaching out over the wire.

"WHEN ALL THE CLOCKS BREAK, TIME GOES ON WITHOUT THEM"

Michael Blumenthal

The clocks have stopped
in this quiet house,
there are no deadlines,
the diary's full of plans
crossed out, postponed
until things change.

I clean my teeth and
make the bed, cook
meals, put washing
out to dry, write
something new.

Time goes on regardless.

children and parents
work on line,
share screens
and give each other
elbow room.
Spurts of rage and fear
erupt at times;
not every house is calm,
all children safe.

Delivery drivers
pound the motorways,
workers in gloves stack
supermarket shelves,
nurses do shifts that
drive them to their knees,
then sleep and start again.

UNREALITY BECOMES REALITY.

People reach deep inside themselves,
find new and unexpected things.
Days grow warmer, I hear birdsong
when I walk outside. Soon there'll be
ducklings on the pond, seedlings
will be ready to be planted out.

TILL THE NEW GROWTH COMES

The horses are working their way
through the bale, finding in the hay
a memory of grass, a lingering taste
of oxeye daisies, corncockle, clover –
fanciful perhaps, but flavour of a sort is there.

And we get through the dry stuff of our days.
We talk at a safe distance, phone our friends,
we zoom, send email hugs, share jokes.
We pull love from the bale and scatter it,
it keeps us going till the new growth comes.

DON'T SPRAY THE WEEDS

What can you do when the well's so deep
your bucket can't reach water, clouds are
indifferent wisps of nothing, making
no shape you can play with, the hole
in your life's so big it's an effort to
open your eyes and get out of bed?

But you do. You wash your face, drink
your tea, eat something. Outside in the yard
a dandelion's forced its way through the tarmac
and come into bloom. Today you will message
a friend, add a smiley face and a flower.

THE CRACK WILLOW

It must have happened in the night:
the split in the trunk had been
widening all winter, little by little
the calloused weather-beaten bark
cracking, torn muscle ripping apart.

This morning sunlight circles
a shadow dance of dark and light
through fallen limbs, wind plays
with an upright branch or two,
the rest lie twisted out of shape,
splayed in the dirt.

If I could put my ear against the tree,
I'd hear the heartwood beat; sap
still runs, leaves will appear, a limb
or two will root into the soil.

In the distance a child laughs, singing
carries on the breeze. A man with a dog
calls across the field, asks me how I am.
We talk about our dogs, our splintered lives,
feel better when we go our solitary ways.

LOOKING AT NOTHING, SEEING EVERYTHING.

An ancient oak with branches like bleached coral
stands foursquare in the centre of the field.
The bare bones of my view - a water trough,
fence-posts, a barn roof, a gate on the skyline.

Yesterday a fawn fled like glancing sunlight
along the boundary. This morning a man plods
up the slope, opens the gate, lopes out of sight.
Two dogs run in circles, then race after him.

Closer, a pair of magpies strut and stab the soil,
a pigeon waddles in mud, a heron powers overhead,
long legs trailing. I watch shape-shifting clouds paint
drifting shadow patterns on the land.

Insignificance becomes significant. These long days
I notice things I overlooked before. I'll tread the earth
with tenderness when this is past, I'll value
 every sunrise, every sunset, every ordinary day.

REALITY CHECK

In the wardrobe, shoes sit
quietly in pairs, a winter coat
rubs shoulders with a fleece,
a yellow dress flounces for attention.

I look at last year's memories
and this year's busy plans.
The coat came out for Midnight
Mass, stilettos at New Year,
the yellow dress is still unworn.

So many things are unimportant now,
my life's drilled down to bedrock:
food, shelter, warmth and love,
what more do I need?

'LOVE ONE ANOTHER AS I HAVE LOVED YOU'

It's a strange Easter; we walk through Holy Week,
together but alone, feeling the sun on our skin,
seeing rebirth everywhere.

And I remember Monet's blood-red field,
a mother and a child half-hidden in waist-high grass,
wading through poppies, wind and clouds overhead,
butterflies and insects round them, above - nothing but air.

Everywhere kindness is springing up like
poppies in a stony field; neighbour to neighbour
stranger to stranger, simple imaginative acts of love
softening the soil, spreading a blaze of colour like shed blood.

IN LIMBO, EASTER SATURDAY

It's the day after He died.

I try to picture it -
that strange half-light
when everything's unreal
there's no-where safe to stand
grief shivers in an icy fog
alone, afraid, waiting.

I feel it,
here in my room
alone, waiting.

EASTER DAY

Last year it was dawn when we walked empty streets,
lit candles, carried them into the dark church,
sat and listened to the Easter story, waited till
the east window blazed with light, then
hugged and breakfasted together.

This year we sit in quiet kitchens, bedrooms,
living rooms, hear the familiar words echoing
down an empty aisle, or from a living room,
a kitchen smelling of toast. This is Easter
stripped back to bone; no incense, vestments,
gold and silver, just light strengthening
till it blazes out of the blackest of places.

SEEDLINGS

Some are thin as a breath,
hooks for the light to catch
and lift, a steady push-pull
out of claggy ground.

Others raise green snouts
snuffing the air, shouldering
their way through sifted soil,
fleshy leaves oiled in sunshine.

Roots squeeze through cracks, tunnel
under tarmac, scramble over rocks,
feel their way forward with the tips
of fingers, grip the earth.

When grief floods my face,
 if I can anchor myself, harness
that blind strength, the will
 to go on reaching for the light,

then buds will swell, and crumpled
leaves will open wide.

CLIMBING THE HILL

We climb the hill,
sit on the bench
with its memorial plaque,
look down at the
huddle of homes,
the hump-backed
bridge over the canal,
the pub with its bright
baskets of pansies.

From up here it looks
as it has always done,
sun sparking Sally's skylight,
silvering the holly hedge.

But it's too quiet. No-one
sits outside the pub, or
walks along the lane.
A solitary figure hangs
washing on a line. Two
doors up someone's
bent over, weeding.
No voices carry on the wind,
no cars pass, the train runs
empty.

This little world is side-lined;
safe for now, but day by day
the cost that we must pay
is rising.

WALKING THE TOWPATH IN RAIN

It's 7am my boots squelch in mud,
water drips from branches overhead, rolls
off my hood, turns the dog's fur to string.

The canal's a tarnished mirror pitted
with rain. Two sleeping swans drift like
soft white pillows. A moorhen chugs past.
A narrowboat's moored on a bend
with a notice on a shuttered window
asking for cotton sheets to make scrubs.

On the bank two plastic chairs, a child's
pink trampoline, a brimming dog bowl.
All the way home a story rolls between
my fingers like a worry-stone.

REFLECTIONS

The canal's mirror-bright today,
shows me the underside of things;
 a coke can caught in an alder's roots,
a pink bootie flowering in the sedge,
a fishing float dangling from a branch;

the upside-down-ness of familiar things
floating out of reach. I teeter carefully
between what's real and what I glimpse
beneath the surface of my life.

I plan my day, treadmill of chores,
on-screen work and calls to make.
I stop and watch the clouds, learn
to let time trickle through my fingers,
feel the texture of each tiny grain.

BALSAM POPLARS

Buds are breaking on the poplar trees,
young leaves gleam with lip-gloss, spice the air;
the scent of balsam's like a tune I love, but
can't quite place, coming and going on the wind.

I love these spring-time cottonwoods, rub
their bark, rough skin against rough skin,
look up the towers of leaf-light planted
as whips; pencils pushed in the ground,
writing the future.

Poplar fluff drifts across empty parks,
gathers on grandstands, around benches.
Feather-light laughter catching, lifting,
catching and lifting, ethereal voices
swirling across continents and oceans.

I breathe in the aroma, swung in a censer
like a prayer.

BOOKING A SUPERMARKET DELIVERY

You are held in a queue
a stick figure
on a green path
is always at the point
where the green ends.

The ribbon unreels
behind him, ahead
is faint and undefined,
he strides steadily, never
changing pace.

It's mesmerising,
minutes drop
one by one.
I can't see who's
ahead of me, only
fleshless numbers
vanishing.

I want to scream
we're more than
walking symbols
on a screen
we smile
we speak
we trip
we fall
someone
comes
picks us up
we carry on.

GREEN

Each day I walk this little wood
in shifting light and shade among
the slow unfurling of green thoughts.

My feet crack fallen branches, scuff
leaf-litter into dust. Overhead
oak trees are a haze of foxy flowers
but the ash are sick, leafless twigs
scratch the sky. They're dying.

Around me everything is green,
spathes of jack-in-the pulpit, sorrel,
comfrey and fat bluebell leaves.

Only the ash are grey, the ground
beneath them bare. No green will
come, no keys will spiral down
in Autumn gales. I grieve for them,
for all who die before their time.

A BIRTHDAY PROMISE

In the photograph you sit straight-backed,
hands neatly folded in your lap,
your children and grandchildren
ranged around you, great-grandchildren
cross-legged on the grass.

Today you're in your room,
wearing comfortable clothes,
eating a solitary meal.

We'll climb the walls that keep you safe,
sit on the top and wave to you.
We'll lower our love in a basket,
put in birthday cards, crayon drawings,

homemade gifts, and stories, send
long distance hugs and smiles on screen,
singing and laughter on the line,
and when we have to go, we'll leave
a row of tea-lights shining in the dark.

KEEPING IN TOUCH

Two small figures sit in sunlight
at the top of the field

too far away for songs or sadness
to carry on the wind.

Disembodied voices swarm
like midges on lake water,

words hatched in hollow rooms buzz
the interweb, decisions roll like dice,

lives lost, lives saved, counted,
costed, - roll the dice again.

The field's in shadow now, the couple
leave. They wave and I wave back

a semaphore of hopes and fears
until they're out of sight.

VERTIGO

I dream
the falling dream
see
thick, muscled arms
your arms
your hand
reaching out
across the void
another
mine
stretching out
straining to grasp it
fingertip to fingertip
a breath apart

a longing
a sickness

as deep
as the two metres
I must keep away
from you.

inspired by Michelangelo's painting in the Sistine Chapel of God creating Adam

WHAT'S A SAFE DISTANCE?

Boundaries are chalked on pavements,
queues staked out and monitored.

We learn the dance for supermarket aisles,
railway platforms, footpaths, country lanes,

steps carefully choreographed,
we wait our turn, judge our distances:

further than breath meeting breath,
beyond hand-stretch to hand-stretch.

I watch two ponies among buttercups
grooming each other, lying side by side.

The collie's head is heavy on my foot,
I run my fingers through her fur, feel

the warmth of her.

SECRET GARDENS

The towpath sneaks past
hedges thick with ivy,
doors hidden in green shadows.

I step into a snicket
to let a runner pass,
lean against a fence.

Through a broken slat
I glimpse a compost bin,
a wheelbarrow, a spade,

mown grass, a trike,
trays of seedlings
ready to be planted out:

no click of shears,
crunch of gravel
under heavy boots,

no voice humming
a tune, everything
on hold, waiting.

I hug the margins of
my life, wash my hands
when I get home.

SOIL UNDER MY FINGERNAILS

I'm planting a new garden,
easing lavender and rosemary from plastic pots,
teasing out tangled root-threads, combing
them into sifted soil, firming them in place.

I've time to be more patient now, no need
to tug at knots in Kate's long hair
before the school bus comes, tease out
the root of Tom's clenched silences.

I'm living at the pace of plants,
firming my roots into the patient earth,
letting the healing come.

LIFTING LOCKDOWN

The wind's strong at the top of the field
acres of buttercups flicker in heat and light.
Birches shift and hassle on the margins.
A slate sky hardens the horizon. Air
sizzles with impatience, the motorway
roars like surf on shingle.

I take the slow way down, grass flattened
underfoot - not ready to outrun my fears.

THE PHOTOGRAPH

There we are; all of us,
arms around waists,
shoulder to shoulder,
squinting in the sun,
squashed in to fit the
frame, hugger-mugger,
happy and smiling.

Next time we meet, we'll laugh and reminisce,
grateful to be together. There'll be no photograph
to fit our scattered lives into a frame.

Chess pieces on a board,
we occupy two metre squares.
We learn new moves,

but we weren't meant to be apart.
Like wrens who huddle in a ball
when winter comes, we need
a hand to squeeze,
arms around us,
keeping out the cold.

RESPITE

Gaia is shaking off lice
licking herself clean like a cat
twisting and turning to get at the
burrowing teeth, the clinging dirt.

For a few short weeks the world
went quiet, the sky was blue
over Beijing, air smelled sweet
in Kolkata, at Heathrow and Gatwick
flocks of planes settled on runways.

I hear a cuckoo, the ping of a
bicycle bell, walk home safely
in the middle of the road, long
for it all to last a little longer.

HARBOUR

The water's quiet here, sheltered
by the sea wall. Slop and slap
of waves is distant, muted,
muffled by weathered granite.

Beached boats settle on their sides,
a stream trickles quicksilver beads
between rocks, two gulls
squabble and tear at a dead fish.
A figure stands, squinting into the sun,
watches the horizon.

Swell rolls
like a thick muscle
against the harbour wall,
heavy with a scum of sorrow.

WHAT WILL IT BE LIKE WHEN WE GET THERE?

It's a long, uncertain journey
a map with lines scored
through flimsy paper
a wheezing
climb up
tightly-packed
contours
a scree-slip
struggle
over a high pass
cloud closing in,
glimpses of blue sky
a slow descent
step by careful step
picking a way over
rock-fall and rubble
to a footpath through
a field of broken lives
fallen waymarks
barbed wire,
boot-prints in mud
a track widening
levelling out
familiar landmarks
places we know well
finding ourselves home
but changed.

WOOL-GATHERING

There's something unstoppable
in the slide of clouds,

wind-quarried, roiling shapes
roll across acres of sky.

My thoughts fray, form and re-form,
dissolve into nothingness.

The day swings on its mooring;
the tide begins to turn.

UNLOCKING

How will it be when I remove
the chain, swing the door wide,
let out the sour smell of fear,
squeeze past the piled up clutter
of frustration, step outside,
soft-skinned and wary of the world?

A hermit crab, crimped too tight,
risking un-shelling on the trampled sand,
where will I find a settling?

SAPLING

A bud, a leaf, a thread of root;
a seedling hope I firm into the earth,
water when shadows come.

Each day the harsh light
hammers it, heat sears
its leaves, the soft stem wilts.

Each night it knits
deeper into the earth, its
heartbeat strengthens.

I watch for the promise
of slow greening,
a glimpse of blossoming,
bee-humming days.

PLEASE WAIT WHILE WE TRY TO RECONNECT YOU

We have cloth voices now,
our words are muffled
when we meet on trains
in hospitals and shops.

Our eyes are eloquent, they
speak the language of a smile,
the grief trapped in a trembling lip.

We've lost the comfort of a hug,
cool fingers on a sun-flushed cheek,
a hand on a bowed head.

Phones and screens are fleshless
substitutes, but we weren't made for this,

longings will leak through every crack,
burst every barrier we make,
find a fresh way through.

EYE TO EYE

Van Gogh yellow from the top of the slope
to the gate, the field is screaming dandelions -
and then the shouting dies away,

nothing left but scattered puffs of breath,
ghost faces among whispering grasses,

and when I kneel among them, eye to eye
I see hieroglyphs of light and air, fragile
parachutes of hope.

BIRTHDAY PRESENT

He brought me his new truck
still in its box, unpacked it carefully,
showed me how the trailer fitted,
placed it on the table between us.

Granny, look but you mustn't touch

Bear-hugs and cuddles hang
in the air between us. We share
smiles and funny faces, jokes
and make-believe stories.

At night I dream his weight against
my shoulder, his moth- breath on my cheek
wake with a lump of loneliness
lodged deep inside.

AFTERWARDS

The padlock's gone from the farm gate,
the Covid warnings taken down. Cars queue
on the motorway slip road.

In the new houses, Ben checks tires and oil,
wipes dust and dead flies off the windscreen,
shakes out the mats.

Jane packs lunchboxes, makes toast,
the twins bicker over breakfast. After they leave
she goes to her work-station, turns on her screen,

beside her on the desk, a mug of coffee
sits untouched.

ACKNOWLEDGEMENTS:

These poems are some of the 94 poems written one a day during lockdown. Thank you, my many friends and neighbours for your encouragement and your comments as the days dragged on. It gave the poems a life and a voice.

Jenna Plewes studied English at Durham University, changed to Social Studies at Edinburgh University. She trained in Medical Social Work, then psychotherapy, working in Hospital and in General Practice. She feels she has come full circle, returning to the writing she sidelined while bringing up her family. Her poems appear in magazines and a number of anthologies. She has published a pamphlet and 5 collections, the latest, *The Salt and Sweet of Memory* published by Dempsey and Windle in 2019. *A Woven Rope*, published by V.Press comes out later this year. She and her husband live in Worcestershire with their border collie. They have 2 children and 4 grandchildren.

Jenna was the joint winner of the Hedgehog Press 'Full Fat Collection Competition' in 2020 and will be donating the proceeds from the sale of the book to the Samaritans and Childline.

ISBN 978-1-913499-44-0

90000

9 781913 499440

www.hedgehogpress.co.uk